Yes Lord, I Hear Your Call

A Prayer Journal for those Answering
the Divine Call to Prayer and Intercession

Dr. Deirdre M. Leaks

Divine Works Publishing, LLC.

© 2024 Dr. Deirdre M. Leaks
Yes Lord, I Hear Your Call

All rights reserved. No part of this publication may be reproduced, stored in a retrieval system, or transmitted in any form or by any means, electronic, mechanical, photocopying, recording or otherwise without the prior permission of the publisher or in accordance with the provisions of the Copyright, Designs, and Patents Act 1988 or under the terms of any license permitting limited copying issued by the Copyright Licensing Agency.

The views expressed in this work are solely those of the author and do not necessarily reflect the views of the publisher, the publisher hereby disclaims any responsibility for them.

ISBN-13: 978-1-949105-64-3 (paperback)

First Edition Published: 03/06/2024
Printed in the United States

Published by:
Divine Works Publishing
Royal Palm Beach, Florida USA
561-990-BOOK (2665)

www.DivineWorksPublishing.com

Dedication

In Memory of a few beautiful and profound women who deeply impacted my life:

Mrs. Willie Mae Reid

Mrs. Annie Mae Willis

Mrs. Tommie Jewel Thomas

Mrs. Lou Ellis Ponder

Mrs. Stella Mae Dukes

Mrs. 1st Lady Gloria Jean Fuller

Minister Mercer Akins

Apostle Evelyn Ponder

Yes Lord, I Hear Your Call
Contents

Introduction 7

I. SPRING 9

II. SUMMER 31

III. FALL 65

IV. WINTER 81

A Note From the Author 92

About the Author 93

Acknowledgements 95

Introduction

Whatever season is before you, allow prayer to proceed from your lips.
- Dr. Deirdre Leaks

Shhhhhh... Who told you to be quiet? Don't be silenced in your outcry to the Lord. Words, phrases, yearnings, and declarations come together to develop our prayers to the Lord. Our communication in prayer is vital for survival.

Whatever season is before you, allow prayer to proceed from your lips. Prayer is an intimate time where we surrender our all, yielding complete dependency upon the Lord Jesus Christ.

During this specific prayer journey, which I share within the pages of this book, I experienced the amazement of our Savior! I was able to habitat in Him and have been overwhelmed by His immense mercy. This six-month prayer journey, spanning from May to November, aligned perfectly with the changing seasons.

Seasons come to navigate us through life. They are necessary for us to truly experience our existence. Whether you prefer the freshness of Spring, the warmth of Summer, the beauty of Fall, or the serenity of Winter, seasons remain constant; regardless of their duration, they invite us to engage with God's magnificent creation.

My time of daily prayer is the breath of my life. I arise early that I may sit in His presence and listen with utmost attentiveness. My prayer time is a daily habitation where I yearn greatly for more of our Savior. It is an intimate time where His IMPARTATION revives my all. Call Him, Listen to Him, Obey Him, REMAIN. I surrender completely and proclaim, "YES LORD. I HEAR YOUR CALL!"

It is an honor that everyday I have another opportunity to lay before Him and release my all. My places of despair but yet places of bloom; my places of distraught but yet places of bursting light; my places of fear but yet places of needful change; the cold places of iniquity but yet places where new life is emerging forth. Those places, those seasons have launched me into a fervent abounding intercession in God. Every season is crucial that we may emerge into the next dimension in our lives. Enjoy your seasons for His beauty awaits your arrival.

Psalm 66:18 If I regard iniquity in my heart, the Lord will not hear me: 19 But verily God hath heard me; he hath attended to the voice of my prayer. 20 Blessed be God, which hath not turned away my prayer, nor his mercy from me.

SPRING

SPRING

The freshness of Spring represents growth and life merging forth abundantly. As we launch into this new season let us not resist the purity of hope knocking on our door.

LET US PRAY

Dear Lord, Our Father and Savior, we exalt your name. We humbly come before you to express our gratitude for the freshness and abundance of Spring. It is a season of growth and new life, and we open our hearts to embrace the purity of hope that knocks on our door.

As we embark on this new season, we pray for your guidance and presence in our lives. Help us to expect great things from you and to fully embrace the opportunities for flourishing that lie ahead. You are mighty and always mindful of your children, and we willingly submit to your will.

We thank you for the gift of this new day, and we stand ready to leap into this journey with enthusiasm, declaring our heartfelt response, "Yes, Lord, I hear your call."

*In your loving and powerful name, we pray.
Amen.*

I. SPRING

I'm a spring leaf trembling in anticipation.
- Maya Angelou

May 3

To abide in your presence is the greatest fulfillment. Vacation is good, choice food is good, spending time with my family is good but my habitation in the Lord produces greatness. It's a pure delight to set everything aside and just be captured by you. You're my Creator. You're my Deliverer. You're my Joy. You're my Peace. You're my all. Nobody has to command me to call on you. **I come with great anticipation because of YOU!**

May 4

As you pray, I'm coming for my words. As for me, I will call upon the name of the Lord and God will save me. Morning, noon and evening will I cry and the Lord shall hear me. (Psalm

55:15-16) Prayer pleases ME. Sometimes a hairstyle or food or money in the bank pleases you. But seeing you call ME, pleases ME. Come to ME in assurance that I am able and I will see you through. As you arise, are you thinking of ME? Praying to ME, allows your thoughts to be voiced to ME.
Prayer challenges and changes.

May 5

Your atmosphere is life changing. I seek to get in your presence that I may experience you. Not just a shiver or a jerk but a real experience of you. Who else can I communicate with that changes my life eternally? I want to know the deepness of you. My prayer to you is so personal. It's my most intimate place that I yearn for greater everyday. Praise stills the enemy. Prayer still and steals the enemy. Do you need him to be still? Do you want to repossess what he has tried to capture? You can in prayer!
In talking to ME I still and steal your adversary.

May 6

Rejoice in knowing to pray. I watch as you come and lay before ME. Anticipate the voice of my release. Let your yearnings in ME, be daily intensified. Stagnation should never be in prayer. Worship and adoration for ME should always be combined with your prayer. I have called you to this place of prayer. Be saturated in ME. Once small children begin to talk, their vocabulary usually increases.
In my presence are your prayers increasing? YES, LORD.

May 7

Pray, pray, pray. As a born again believer, this should take priority. Other voices should never be your option. Laying

out before ME should always be your place of refuge. As you pray expect an encounter. Praying is not a ritual or a forceable routine but a place of safety where you come to learn of ME. **I hear my children praying. Come in.**

May 8

Prayer prevents. Prayer propels. Prayer prospers. Prayer purges. Prayer penetrates. Prayer pursues. Prayer pains. Prayer produces. Who can live in ME without prayer? I take delight in your daily fellowship. I see your yearnings and groans that deliverances will come forth. Search ME and allow my words of life bring you to continual elevation. **I commit to dispersing my answers.**

May 9

Pray in the morning, pray at night. Stay ready to pray. I have called everyone to pray but where's the effort? Where is that place of consistency? Where is that place where you have given ME complete access? In that place of prayer, don't hold back. I want you to pray because you love ME. I want you to pray because you see countless needs. I want you to pray knowing that I am able! **Pray unto ME, for I take delight in seeing your total surrenderance. Pray.**

May 10

Prayer protects. Cry out to ME that my hand will remain upon you. Many things come before you. Look for ME for the change and believe ME for the release. Praying should never be your last option but the place you come first. Praying to ME disciplines you in your wait. Be anxious for nothing but in all things in prayer and supplication, let your requests be made known. **What did you say?**

May 11

It's time to pray. When? All the time. It's time to exalt the name of the Lord! Keep a forever excitement in your prayers. My ears are attentive, keep declaring ME and stay in expectation of ME. You can't ever let doubt traumatize you. In believing ME you receive your assured peace.
Distractions comes when you pray, keep praying.

May 12

Pray persistently. Prayer pulls. As I reveal, keep prayer prevalent. Pray not according to what you see but pray believing ME. I have put an unction in you to pray in all things. Prayer goes before you and prepares your God-ordained destiny. Who tells you not to pray? Satan takes delight in your silence.
Pray my child and believe ME.

May 13

Praying in ME, releases a praise from you to ME. Why do you pray? Its our intimate time together. It's the time where pureness is pulled from your lips to come to my ears. Why is it time to pray? It is certainly time to get in that most intimate place. Pray with my loving compassion and joy.
It is always time to pray.

May 14

Did you hear my call? Did you hear my request for Intercession? Let it delight you to get in this place. This place where your healing comes and remain. This place where every stronghold is dismantled and every generational curse is destroyed. Yes, I have called you to this place of greatness. This is my place where I mold you. This is my place where I purge you.
This is my place. Welcome. Abide!

May 15

The benefits to praying are everlasting. It's not a routine but an adoration for ME. It's this place where you want to be seared by my word. I want you to pray. I want you to be assured of my might. I parted the Red Sea with my great might. I spoke let there be light and it came forth. The atmosphere was perfect for ME to prevail. Be purged in ME and totally dependent in ME. **Pray my child and expect.**

May 16

Did you pray? It's not an option but a place that you should resort to daily. Prayer brings understanding. As you pray in ME, you'll receive my thoughts on the matter. I want you to pray. I want you to call on my name. You are not clueless for I provided my detailed direction in prayer. **Come and pray with ME and stay awhile.**

May 17

Isn't it a time to pray? In your fasting and prayer, it brings a total surrenderance unto ME. You become my sponge and I want you to soak up my every fiber. When you pray to ME, I respond. I don't leave you in despair. Some in class are ready to learn. You are in that place where you want more. In prayer, your cravings and appetite are unquenchable. **Pray no matter the temperature. Pray no matter the request. Pray.**

May 18

Did you hear ME say pray? Did you hear ME say release it? Did you know that I am hearing you? Praying to ME, builds and strengthens our relationship. How can you be fully connected when you are doubtful of what I say?

Patiently await my release. Anticipate my manifestation. Stay in this place of surrenderance and don't be moved. **I want your prayer to intensify greater that your every prayer is consumed from ME.**

May 19

Did I quicken you to pray? Did you feel ME nugging at your heart? Freely come into my presence. Find yourself stilling away in ME. Put everything aside that you may hear ME clearly. I want you to have a crisp reception. The more you sit in ME the clearer you'll understand my direction. It's a delight to see you delight in ME. Come to pray. Come to dwell. **Come sit in, ME that I may sit in you. Pray always.**

May 20

As you pray, I'm looking inside of you. I want you to release your every care and not holding on to anything. Prayer channels the journey for complete victory. Don't you feel better after you express yourself? Thats why you should always pray. I want you to talk to ME, so I can respond. Who Prays? Those that know I am the releaser. Those that know I am present. Pray seeking to dwell in that intimate sacred place. Do you ever consider praying? **Do you believe in my releasing power? Yes Lord.**

May 21

I do want all men to pray. I want them to get in their appointed time and lay out before ME. Come to the call! Come to the place where I mend your heart. Come to the place where I take out the uncleanliness and wash you thoroughly. Come to the place where I mold you into my likeness. Isn't this the place you yearn for? This is the place where my hands are extended to you. **Come. Pray!**

May 22

Did you hear ME? You did. For I said it's time to pray and you came. You didn't look at anything but what I said. It is time to pray. It's time to launch. My word is to be learned, applied and walked thoroughly. I have never told you to give up and quit. The enemy delights in failure but I come with my supernatural SUCCESS. I give seed to seed. I make deposits in you to seed out. If you don't pray you'll lack my timing of dispersing. Pray believing. Where is the PAYOFF? **It's coming forth through your prayer and obedience.**

May 23

Who told you not to pray? I said pray without ceasing. I said men ought to always pray and faint not. Prayer reaches continually. There is a need. Rejoice in being able to see the purpose of prayer. When you pray to ME, I focus on you. I reveal in prayer. Don't waste time in the negative but be assured in my wonder working prayer. I want your time. I don't ever want it to be absorbed with the tactics of Satan. Pray my daughter and don't look back. **For you have conquered what's behind you. Pray.**

May 24

I love for you to pray. Prayer settles the atmosphere. Prayer provides the path for a clear journey. When you pray, pray with your all. Pray believing my word. I express myself in my word that you may visualize it and grasp its entirety. Whatever you look at, look at it with deep prayer. Without hesitation of its outcome but delighted that prayer brings forth victory. How do you pray? You open your mouth, visualize ME and experience my presence. **You pray and I prevail.**

May 25

Pray at all times. Satan is the only one that tells you not to pray. He doesn't want you to overcome anything. Your prayers propel you to ME. I am able to manifest in the core of your soul when you pray. Pray not because I told you, but because you want more of ME. I am coming into your prayers and making habitation. When you see others pray, pray with them. They are trusting ME and it's what I expect from all of my children. Who told you not to pray? It wasn't ME. I told you to come before the throne room of grace boldly! **Let us pray.**

May 26

Pray, pray, persist. This is the season where you shall have unquenchable prayer. Situations, negative or positive should never affect your prayer. I am calling forth this elevation. I want this place to always be set aside. All can pray but some won't enter in. I take delight in seeing this time set aside. Who called you to pray? I called you to pray and I'm calling you to continual prayer. **Pray my daughter, pray.**

May 27

I called you to pray. I called you and you responded. The call is for everyone, but everyone doesn't answer. In class some just come and some actively participate. I take delight in seeing you activate my word. Prayer prepares you for activation of my word. I don't want you to be ever stuck in prayer but I want you to come out of all barriers. When I call you to pray, I'm exchanging. You are giving ME your application and I am coming in with full capacity. In prayer, I do want you to absorb all of ME. Pray for this season, never stop nor become stale. **You become renewed in ME as you open your mouth. Pray.**

May 28

Pray when? There is always a time to pray. While others are speaking, pray. As you pray, then speak. You set the atmosphere for my wisdom to prevail. Prayer is an essential asset and necessity in my kingdom. Banker's deal with money and prayer warriors deal with prayers. Don't rush to judgement but pray so that you can give sound wisdom. Let your prayers come up before ME.
Teach others to pray. Be my prayer example.

May 29

Being grateful stands up before ME. Conqueror in my word as you pray. As you pray, your praise and thanksgiving comes up before ME. You just don't pray but you set the atmosphere for ME to habitatate. Praying set many things in order. The call to prayer is great but the surrenderance to come is greater. As a little girl, I sat you down to hear your great grandmother pray. Not much education but a great heart to pray to ME. She yearned in the spirit and the yearnings continue today.
Pray. The yearnings will continue from you.

May 30

There is so much to prayer. As you see souls in your midst, pray. We can look at the need and pray. Lord teach us to be a knee meeter. If you don't pray, you won't be sensitive of what's before you. There are times when you seed the need and go forth in intercession. Be alert continually and be in that place where you stay on ready. Every level you achieve in prayer, I want more. Prayer does wonders for your focus in ME. Send prayer afar off. Send prayer in the current. Pray when you're beginning the race, in the midst of the race and when you're right at the finish line.
Pray my daughter. It's contagious!

May 31

It's a time to pray. This is a time to call on ME like never before. I am touching that tender place that you will mount up in ME. Strength comes through prayer. Calling on ME advances you. Some hear the call to pray and go in a different direction. As you hear my call, yield, obey and reproduce. Pray in all things. My wisdom remains in you as you consistently pray. I have never told you not to pray. **Pray and then pray again.**

June 1

Prayer is continual and rises higher in ME. It lightens your life when you lay everything down before ME. You don't have to be in that place where you're entangled with situations. Lay all things at my feet. I called you to pray and you heard ME. As you heard the call, receive the released answers. I have put you all in a deep forest and I'm cutting the path to victory. Stay on the trail of righteousness. Pray when it's not clear to you and I will give you direction. **What does it cost you to pray? An intimate time in ME.**

June 2
PRAYING.

June 3

Pray in all things. Nothing can stand up against the power of prayer. Prayer sets, then I come in and overtake. Whatever Satan wants to do, prayer stops him. Sincere prayer brings ME forth in manifestation. I want my intercession to come forth mightily. It has a great uniqueness. In your prayers believe my every word. **Pray that my strength will always overshadow you. Pray.**

June 4

Praying is crucial. As you come to ME, I hear the sincerity of your heart. I see the pulls but I see your prayers. We go to jobs, salons, cell carriers, doctors, grocery stores; many places that we have established good history. You have established praying. Other things are subject to change In a moment but what you have established in prayer and your consistency lasts your life. Pray and pray with reverence. Pray believing. **Pray knowing. Pray rejoicing. Pray!**

June 5

Did you hear ME? I said let us pray. Signifying you are not alone. As you trust to come to ME, trust to know that "I am" is present. In your prayers you have to say, what I have said. Your credit card doesn't activate by looking at the sticker. You have to use effort to get access. There aren't restrictions, just surrender. Don't you know you have prayer power but don't refuse to use it. Many pray for different reasons but pray because I am your first option. Pray because you love what I say regardless.
Pray for the harvest and journey before you.
Pray my daughter.

June 6

Prayer goes afar off. Pray and expect ME. Always expect the unexpected. Pray and let my rain overtake you. Pray and know I am present and disregard other things. Life is full of dilemmas but you must always let ME prevail. I want you to continue to increase in prayer. I'm nurturing you in prayer.
Prayer rains without restrictions.

June 7

Come in to pray. Prayer is intimate and brings you closer to ME and my word. Prayer takes your attention from the negative that you tune in wholly to ME. I Don't want you to pray with your lips but to be consumed in your heart. In your prayers, give it all to ME. Pray and believe ME without any hesitation. Some may say they are praying but I'm available to those that really pray. **My daughter in all things, pray and rejoice knowing I release the ordained victory! Pray.**

June 8

When my prayer resides in your soul, nothing can stop you from praying. You pray as you arise, you pray in what's revealed to you. You pray as you lie down and then as you begin again, you are still praying. Some people know the importance of prayer and some are scared to enter in. Come to ME in prayer that I'll cleanse you and keep your prayer fluent. Prayer releases my promises from thine mouth into the heavenly for manifestation.
Pray... and then pray again.

June 9

Praying is crucial to the life you live. Prayers go forth to set up and arrange what's to come. Praying should be a priority. Not to be considered a routine, but instead a great delight to walk into such a surrendered place. This place where I'm open to all your heartaches and questions. This place where I see deeply into you. Come to this place of prayer that I may talk to you. Your coming destroys division and brings my everlasting hope.
Come and pray in ME.

June 10

Pray. Whether the sun or the storm, pray. Whether hot or cold, pray. Whether thick or thin, don't ever let prayer pass you by. Many know to pray but refuse to get in this place of surrenderance. Prayer changes you, when you ignore everything else. Why should you pray? Yes, it will take you to the place of maturity. Yes, prayer will destroy those intense generational strongholds. When prayer is on the inside of you, there is no room for hesitation of my will. There is no room for idle thoughts to get in. Pray my daughter and believe ME.
Watch out for my reign!

June 11

Recognizing my voice causes you to move swiftly, because you realize the extreme importance of adhering to ME. Don't ever take for granted that I'll just keep calling. Yes Lord, is sufficient for your journey. This elevation keeps you moving forward until there is no room for delay. The more you pray, the less time you have to analyze. The more you pray, the more I have divine access to your temple.
Pray and rejoice continually in ME.

June 12

It is good to always have a mind set to pray. Sometimes you can't speak on situations but you can always pray. I quickened you to pray for your classmates. Many shall come back to ME. Keep this in prayer. I always want you to be in that place where details are minor but my voice is greater. In prayer you are fulfilling the call of God up in your life. Pray that wherever you go, salvation will come forth.
**When you know to pray, pray and watch for my
Holy Ghost results.**

June 13

There is always a reason for your continual prayers. First of all, pray because I have commanded you. Pray because it a delight. Pray because as you release, I'm pouring into you and into your situation. It is a need to pray in all things. Some people see a need for a lot of things but I want you to always see this need to pray. Don't limit my prayers from you or in your midst. Praying makes you sensitive to my spirit.
Prayer continually prepares you. Pray in delight.

June 14

Pray! Prayer settles yet guide. Praying pushes you in ME. Watch and pray that ye enter not into temptation: the spirit indeed is willing, but the flesh is weak. (Matthew 26:41) The flesh just wants to have a voice. You silence the flesh and let the spirit prevail in you as you pray. In the anointing I've released to you, prayer channels you in my ordained direction. You can't pray and doubt at the same time. Come and pray to ME that you'll always be equipped for this journey. Pray even the more.
Your prayers bring comfort. Pray.

June 15

Pray and stay. I don't always have you to pray and rise. Many times I want you to pray and absorb my voice. You see the need to pray and don't ever loose your sight. Pray and watch ME loose every stronghold. Pray and watch my love overtake the impossibilities. Prayer will cause you to conqueror. Pray my child and look. I have put an urgency in you to pray.
Your reaction should always be to pray. React in ME.

June 16

Prayer pushes beyond your present. Prayer and praise are beneficial. As you pray and believe ME, usually a praise follows. I want you to always pray. Don't ever let this be a place you slack from but let your prayers excel continually. Pray when you're uncomfortable. Pray when you know flesh wants to operate. Pray because you're my vessel that I need to use. When you don't pray then you're not prepared for my visitation.
Pray that I will always habitatate in you. Yes Lord!

June 17

Pray and watch ME. Pray and expect ME. Pray with pureness of heart. Continual prayer causes growth in ME. When you see a red light, it's a given to stop. No analyzing, no movement, but an immediate STOP. I want you to always have a prayer reaction. Let ME be first. Just know there isn't an alternative as my believer. There is no alternative as my chosen vessel.
If I gave you a choice, wouldn't it always be ME?
Pray and be peaceable in ME.

June 18

Prayer comes forth in all times. People look for many options but seeking ME should always be the first option. Not to pray is to look for disaster. Prayer is your best resource. Your daily prayers should go up before ME as a sweet aroma. Never let prayer be your final resort. Praying crumbles the work of satan.
Be found praying.

June 19

To hear the testimonies of others are great but to have your personal encounters are life changing. Always feel the need to pray. Don't allow it to be a cliche. Allow prayer to be released from the purity of your heart. There are some restaurants that have an A-1 rating with you, but oh how much more your experience with ME. **Tell how I have brought you through every-time! Share the gospel continually.**

*Date:*_____

Prayer Notes: _____
_____
_____
_____
_____
_____
_____

*Date:*_____

Prayer Notes: _____
_____
_____
_____
_____
_____
_____

*Date:*_____

Prayer Notes: _____
_____
_____
_____
_____
_____
_____

*Date:*_____

Prayer Notes: _____
_____
_____
_____
_____
_____
_____

*Date:*_____

Prayer Notes: _____
_____
_____
_____
_____
_____
_____

*Date:*_____

Prayer Notes: _____
_____
_____
_____
_____
_____
_____

 I. SPRING

*Date:*_____

Prayer Notes: _____
_____
_____
_____
_____
_____
_____
_____

*Date:*_____

Prayer Notes: _____
_____
_____
_____
_____
_____
_____
_____

*Date:*_____

Prayer Notes: _____
_____
_____
_____
_____
_____
_____
_____

*Date:*_____

Prayer Notes: _____
_____
_____
_____
_____
_____
_____

*Date:*_____

Prayer Notes: _____
_____
_____
_____
_____
_____
_____

*Date:*_____

Prayer Notes: _____
_____
_____
_____
_____
_____
_____

SUMMER

SUMMER

Summer days can be an anticipation of greatness. Rejoicing in being able to see sunny days and hopefulness in the Lord's merciful grace. Enjoying God's freedom and being able to embark upon the great seasons of life.

LET US PRAY

Heavenly Father, as we enter into the season of Summer, we rejoice in the abundance of blessings that lie ahead. We are grateful for the sunny days and the hopefulness that comes from your merciful grace. As we journey through this season, we humbly ask that you guide our steps and fill our hearts with a desire to seek you in all that we do. Help us to keep our hearts open to your teachings and obedient to your direction.

Father, as we learn more about you and your ways, may our lives become a testimony that brings glory to your holy name. Let our every thought, word, and action be a reflection of your love and grace. In our obedience to your voice, may our confession be, "Yes, Lord, I hear your call, and I will obey."

May this Summer season be a time of growth, joy, and freedom as we walk closely with you.
In the name of Jesus, we pray.
Amen.

II. SUMMER

Like a welcome summer rain, humor may suddenly cleanse and cool the earth, the air and you.
-Langston Hughes

June 20

Praying is not a light thing. It's major and it sets apart and sets my environment. Walk into prayer. Never be in that place where you don't think of praying. Your prayers are evidence that I am on your mind. Praying rejects negativity. Both can't reign. The more you pray, negativity has to flee. Praying is your barrier that shields you from Satan's opposition. You know who don't want you to pray and you know who wants to overtake in prayer.
I'm present. Pray always.

June 21

Pray my daughter. However, the enemy wants to maximize, he's minimized in prayer. Prayer goes to those deep places and causes forth my word to come forth. Pray and not faint. I'm working through you as you diligently call upon my name. I'm taking out what don't belong and making continual deposits of myself. Your prayers reach ME as you pray in purity. **Stay on task and don't be moved from thine assignment. Pray my daughter.**

June 22

Prayer proceeds my power; but you have to pursue after ME for my living power. As you pray, take delight in my protection. Praying clears the path for my safety. Praying gives you the urgency to do my will. Prayer separates yet restores. Prayer causes you to leave all the burdens and conquer in ME. **Pray without doubting and your victories shall come forth. Pray and praise always.**

June 23

Prayer chases the bound that freedom will come forth. Do you see your prayer as a gift? It's as pureness of a jewel that you can come to ME and call my name. Always see the privilege of calling upon my name. People look at countless alternatives but I always want to be your first. As much as you pray with your all, I'm releasing with my all. Prayer pulls you closer into my presence. **When I see you pray, I see you surrendering your all. Pray.**

June 24

Pray, that you may know more of ME. I don't ever want you to be distant from ME. As you pray you're brought to the forefront. When you don't pray, you enjoy being on the back end and not being in my presence. The more you pray the more you see the need for more of ME. Being accepted into my glory is promotion. **In your prayers, my directions are being released for your ordained journey.**

June 25

Arise and pray. Praying doesn't bind you but takes you to greater depths in ME. I don't want you to ever get to a place where you look for ME to come one way. As you pray, I'm deciding my point of contact. It could be in your prayers, it could be as soon as you arise, it could be in your fast. It could be in your outreach. It could be in the service. Don't try to bound ME with your perception but be free to receive. Praying causes ME to reside in you. **As you call, I come forth. Arise and pray.**

June 26

Pray and believe ME. If you pray, that's the first step in believing that I can move on your behalf. Don't pray and then try to handle yourself. Pray and let my word work. Praying gives you an assurance that my word is coming forth. Pray and expect. Pray and stand. Pray and be steadfast. Pray and proclaim. Pray and don't procrastinate. **Pray and provoke others to pray.**

June 27

Why pray? To communicate with thine Creator. When you come to ME, You're activating my principles. As you pray you should realize the significance of your personal encounter. I can't make anyone talk to ME but those that come in purity, I hear the call. Praying is your navigation to ME all day long. Praying directs you to my will. You don't ever stop praying, because it draws you closer to ME in all things. Who considers anything without praying? Some. **Praying keeps ME first. Pray my daughter.**

June 28

Praying is powerful. Praying ceases the power of Satan tactics. Praying causes your growth to come forth. Prayer takes time. Many want a lot but give little in prayer. Grow strong in prayer. You see its significance and don't let it get away from you. Prayer develops you for my glory. Pray and release your every need. You can't pray and hold on to issues. You have to pray and give ME everything. Praying assures you in ME. **Pray and don't ever be hesitant about speaking my words.**

June 29

Pray, releasing my words. Pray believing my words. Pray standing in authority. Pray with a praise. Praise in your prayer. Believe that you have conquered. When you pray, intimacy is manifesting. You begin to see the importance of your IMPARTATION. The enemy wants to stop your prayers but I want them to be stronger. All that you see, pray and watch my response. **Pray and receive your victory. Pray my daughter. Pray.**

June 30

Pray and praise in a dynamic mixture. In your prayers, there should be a yet praise. When you pray you have to believe ME followed by a continual praise. As you pray, I'll remove the stony places. I'll take away every unclear thought. Pray and stay at my feet. I want your prayers to always reach ME. Come forth in the pureness of your heart and I will release my answers. Pray without doubting and watch ME come forth.

Pray my daughter.

July 1

Your prayers should be birthed from my words. As you meditate in ME, let my words of life come forth from you. Praying causes ME into the atmosphere to prevail and remain. You can't grasp all that I'm doing but you know my power. Pray and see the fortified wall being built that Satan can never penetrate. Pray and know that there is a great pulling for souls to come in. Pray and expect. Pray and release.

Pray and surrender all. Pray.

July 2

Praying fervently calls for a complete surrenderance. In your prayers You're coming to know ME. Pray in confidence assured that I'm able. Encourage others to pray. Encourage others to seek ME. I am available to receive your cries. In your prayers, I'm present. In your prayers I'm setting, I'm uprooting. I'm taking care of you. Didn't you think to pray or were you clouded by your situations? Take time to pray and not fret.

Pray my daughter.

July 3

Pray and release. Don't pray and walk out in bondage. Allow ME to come in on every aspect. Rejoice knowing I'm forever present to heal. Some things won't be removed out of your life until you pray and leave it with ME. Stand on my word as you pray and expect ME. You are experiencing my supernatural but there is so much more to go along with it. Whatever is before you, see ME. In your prayers, see my righteousness come forth. When you don't pray, you cut off communication with ME. Your life span is interrupted. Pray and conquer in ME. Who told you not to pray? Conqueror my child.

Pray my daughter. Pray.

July 4

Fervent prayer exposes the enemy. When attacks manifest, go into another level of prayer. The enemy can't overtake your house when fervent prayer is going forth. Some people are in war from a distance but I have called you in prayer to be up close and confrontational in warfare. The enemy plots, but you pull down his tactics in prayer. When you're in the war zone, you're not getting prepared. What you have done previously prepares you for the intense battle.

Pray my daughter and look at my reign.

July 5

It always time to pray. Don't ever think you have prayed too much. There is no such thing. Men ought to always pray. Unlimited prayers ought always go forth in a striking combination of prayers and expectation. Why open your mouth to ME if you have already defeated yourself in doubt? When you come to ME and declare my word, I'll come to you with my word.

Fret not and stay focused in your prayers. Praying produces my righteous fruit. Some ask for your prayers simply because they don't know how to pray. **Pray my daughter.**

July 6

Stay in tune and alerted to pray. As you call on ME, expect ME. The enemy always wants you to see his works but your prayers should devour his visions. As you pray stand firmly on what my word says. Declare it without hesitation. As you counsel begin with prayer. As you pray, I am releasing. Esteem others and lift them up in prayer.
Pray my daughter and don't be moved.

July 7

Pray fervently and bind continually. Satan can't give you something that he doesn't have possession over. Come to ME boldly and watch ME come forth. Stay alert and praise without restraints. I'm calling for more and I'm releasing more. In your prayers keep your focus and let ME continue to replenish you.
Prayer takes you to delicate places but I have equipped you.
Rejoice and pray my daughter.

July 8

Pray in faith having an expectation in your belief. Your prayers go behind the scene purging the hard places. At Nacom I saw your commitment and I created an opportunity for your advancement. You pray and I'll create. Man is always limited. I have no limits. Pray in purity and fervency and watch ME come forth with great might. Pray for those that you know and don't know. Keep praying. It is what I have called you to do in every temperature. **Pray my daughter.**

July 9

In your prayers, I'm humbling you. As you pray you see, as Uriah, *"Lord it is ME with unclean lips"*. Every impurity that I bring to sight, I want you to cast forth in prayer. Don't ever hold on to the unproductive. A rotten apple spreads to others. In prayer keep your spirit clean. Pray aggressively for others that my deliverance will come forth. Many struggle between being free and being bound. **Pray my daughter.**

July 10

Prayer presents precious purities in my midst. The flesh doesn't ever want to pray. It always sees an opportunity to deny my will. You conquered continually as you pour out in prayer and make your body subject to my Spirit. Prayer presses to the impossible. Pray believing, pray standing, pray seeking, pray advancing. Pray because I delight in your communication. There is always a time to pray. Hold not back, but go forth in territories proclaiming pure faith. **Pray my daughter.**

July 11

You are called to pray. I have called you to intercession. Know your place and don't come down from it. Pray for it is your purpose and prayer has purpose. Pray and see the miracles. Pray and believe my words. Pray and launch too greater. Pray in all situations. **Pray my daughter and don't let your calling be disrupted.**

July 12

Praying causes your sensitivity to arise. In your prayers speak my word without hesitation. Don't get to the place where you don't feel like speaking my word because as you speak it, it goes

forth to erupt. Roda and the house prayed and amazement came forth. Pray and wait on the amazement. Sometimes you look at tv and say that just tv, it's not realistic. As you pray and release, you're going to say, it's God and there is no other.
Pray my daughter.

July 13

Praying to ME is powerful. Praying propels you to a closer arena in ME. Whatever it looks like, find yourself praying. Praying is the avenue that will lead you to your destination. Pray and expect ME to come forth. If you don't pray, you will not know where to go. If you don't pray, you will be overtaken. Praying pleases the Father. I want you to pray and faint not.
Pray my daughter, earnestly.

July 14
PRAYING.

July 15

The word of prayer has to be in your mouth. It has to be so prevalent, that you pray in all things. Many have been taught or choose everything except prayer. Be my vessel that will always pray. Praying is effective. Prayer reaches. Prayer elevates. Prayer gives you vision and focuses you. Prayer strengthens you that you will be my fervent vessel.
Pray my daughter and don't be detoured.

July 16

Always let your prayers come from a pure place. Pray that I may be pleased in your presence. Pray always desiring my will in all things. Prayer prompts my introduction. As you pray, you're

reviving your faith that you may have my Godly strength to obey my guidelines. In every prayer, see ME coming forth. See ME bringing my explosion. Pray that I can walk in your heart. Praying grants ME forever habitation in your life.
Pray my daughter.

July 17

Pray in all things. Pursuing and worship takes deliverance, when combined. As you present your body in prayer, I come forth to receive of it. You don't have to know a person to pray for them. When I show you the need or you hear of the need, pray. Pray and trust ME for their miracles.
Let your prayers be continual.

July 18

In your prayers, release my words back into ME. In believing ME, believe the power of my words. Prayer and praise is a powerful and lasting combination. Raining in the abundance is connected to your continual surrenderance. You do what I have commanded of you. Prayers reach ME. Don't hesitate, and expect ME. **Pray my daughter.**

July 19

Praying in ME takes you to your spiritual destiny. Praying in the flesh produces nothing. You can start out praying but I take delight in seeing you go to intercession. Intercession invites you into your ordained seat. Take delight in going into the prepared place. Some have a desire to go but refuse to put forth effort to get there. Put forth the effort to receive of your greatness.
Pray my daughter.

July 20
PRAYING.

July 21

Keep prayer and praise combined. Pray no matter the season. Don't ever find yourself in seasonal prayers. Be found in intensified prayer. Pray diligently. Keep your commitment to prayer. It's an honor to pray and it should be shown in thine actions. Never be silenced in prayer.
Pray my daughter.

July 22

Praying guides you in ME. Praying elevates you in ME but sit you down when necessary. Praying reconstructs and builds wholeness. Some people in life get to a place where they think they know my route and don't acknowledge ME. I am God and your route is subject to your unforeseeable conditions.
Prayer prepares you for all seasons. Pray my daughter.

July 23

Keep your desire to pray to ME. As the prayers come up, keep an expectation that my answers will come forth. I don't midst or sprinkle, but I come forth with a mighty reign. In your prayers you're reaching to greatness. Stay in fervent prayer. Your prayers are not for a season but a way of life. Pray through the rain. Pray through the sun. Pray. I depend on you to pray. Faint not and pray. **It's your ordained place and that's to pray. Pray.**

July 24

It's necessary always to pray. If you go in a dark room, a light is necessary to see. The light gives you the assistance to navigate through. Prayer navigates you in all. It brings you to your destiny. Pray with passion. You don't just pray going through the motion but there must be a complete devotion and confidence in my word. Who told you not to pray? The same one that wants your life. Keep praying, it's your declarations in ME.
Pray my daughter.

July 25

Persevere in prayer. Pray and don't prescribe. I am thine creator and as you seek ME, be assured of my presence. Praying brings you to ME that I may consume your cup. My presence brings the fullness of my power. In prayer, as I speak don't deny my voice. On a runway, a plane is expected to launch. In prayer, I expect you to launch. Nothing should hold you back.
Keep moving in ME. Pray my daughter.

July 26

Pray believing that your prayers will reach ME. I take delight in seeing your approach to ME. In every prayer, there is a solution from my word. Your assignment is to be my continual intercessor. Just pray without analyzing. Pray in my strength and believe in my might to come forth. You are seeing prayers answered. Ignite prayer, for I come on the scene as my word is spoken.
Pray my daughter. Pray.

July 27

Men ought to always pray and faint not. Your prayers go deep and bring forth the fertility of the ground. In your prayers stay surrendered. In your prayers always reverence my will. In your prayers don't get weary. In your prayers heed to ME. In your prayers wait patiently. In your prayers, expect, expect, expect. **Pray my daughter.**

July 28

Stay in my place of surrenderance. I want you to always enter into my presence calling on my name. Praying goes so far. Praying causes you not to be opinionated but to be humble. You are going forth. Continue to pray. The nobleman went and believed what I said. You have to believe as you're praying. Pray and don't be moved. Pray and don't loose hope. **Pray and watch the move of God. Pray my daughter.**

July 29

Prayer brings my word from thine mouth. Call on ME with my word. Let my word ignite in you as you call it forth. Prayer takes time. When you sit with ME, don't be hesitant to ask of ME. Pray in all things. Pray for a continual manifestation of ME. In all your prayers believe my word and don't let my word diminish in time. **Pray my daughter. Pray.**

July 30

Expressions of love are shown as you continually call upon ME in prayer. It takes a loving commitment to come and bow down unto ME daily. In every elevation, let not this Surrenderance get away from you. Pray more. There is never a limit to calling on my name. The limit comes when you don't believe ME. Pray continually that every hindrance must go. Mountains will be removed as you trust ME. **Pray my daughter.**

July 31

As you pray, I shall ignite my fire in you. As you see, pray. In your hearing, pray. In your exercise, pray. In every season, pray. Teach others to pray. Tell others to pray. Let them know your strength comes as you pray and trust ME. I don't ever get tired of your prayers. Pray expecting the fire of God to fall. **Pray relying totally upon ME. Pray my daughter.**

August 1

Your prayers travel to ME. Don't waiver in what you believe. In releasing of my answers stay on track. This intercession shall become stronger and greater. Many like to recite but I like to operate in my children. As you pray the ground becomes fertile for my deposits. Stay in fervent prayer that the harvest will come forth and not be detoured. I can declare my harvest forth but the temperature must be productive for my release. **Pray my daughter.**

August 2

Prayer goes beyond the outer. It reaches the depth of a man's heart. Everyday delight in having an experience in ME. I look forward to your surrenderance. As you pray in ME, you will always see the need to stay at my feet. Prayer launches you into my greater, daily. The enemy can't habitat in you when you pray to ME. **Pray my daughter and encourage others to pray continually.**

August 3

In praying I call my treasures of life from you. Pray in assurance knowing that my ears are open to my children. In your prayers go forth in fervency. You don't always know

what you're attacking or what you're reaching. I want the prayers to reach the heart of the wicked that they will come to ME. Praying gives you the ability to be strengthened in ME. Pray my daughter and stop the spears of Satan.
Pray my daughter.

August 4

Prayer pleases ME. To see you come and surrender in expectation of ME, is necessary. I am the one raising and providing. Take delight in your acknowledgement of ME. I am thine Creator, and your prayers create greater reverence towards ME. Pray and grip firmly. Pray and watch carefully. Pray and heed intensely. Pray and compel the fragile. Pray my daughter and speak my words of life with agape love.
Pray my daughter.

August 5

The power of praying moves unmovable mountains. Your prayers have you to stand upon walls of steel yet look for ME to crumble them through prayer. As you experience my presence, you must be assured that your prayers have reached my throne room. You pray and expect. You pray and believe. You pray without fear. Pray for I take delight in being summoned.
Pray my daughter.

August 6

Pray in perseverance. Pray in delight as you communicate with ME. In praying I see the sincerity of thine heart. I develop the heart that my greatness comes forth. If you worked as a doctor, your code is to help regardless. As my prayer warrior, go into fervent prayer just believing ME regardless. Some won't sit in my presence, but let ME always find you, as I call.
Pray my daughter. Pray.

August 7

I have called you to pray in all things. To get ME on an issue, seek ME in prayer. Prayer precedes victory. Prayer brings you the balance to remain on a solid foundation. You don't step on anything frail because you know you will fall through. Your strong foundation is established through your continual prayers. Look, pray and observe again. **There maybe many challenges but as you continue in prayer, deliverances break forth. Pray my daughter. Pray.**

August 8

At my call, pray. As I interrupt, pray. At uncertainties, pray. In happiness, pray. In distress, pray. In anguish, pray. In every season, pray. Be found praying and expecting. In your prayers, I am fulfilling my words of life. You know who tells you not to pray. **Pray my daughter.**

August 9

Pray my daughter and don't be silenced. Pray and don't let distractions detour you. Pray and let my wisdom continually guide you. Pray when you're faced with impossibilities. Pray in the midst of the rain and storm believing that my sunshine always overtakes. Pray without collapsing. I come to strengthen you in your prayers. Some don't want to pray but they want an answer. **Pray and hear. Pray and heed. Pray my daughter.**

August 10

Sincere prayers manifest my glory. Take delight in seeing ME come forth. I come forth in your prayers to give you the direction and comfort needed. Praying gives you the survival skills for daily life. Pray that you won't become prey. The enemy sees when your spiritual tools are sharpened and when they are dull. Be fervent in your prayers. As your eyes open, go forth in prayer. **My daughter this shall be a time when praying is intense. Pray my daughter. Pray.**

August 11

I am calling you higher. Don't get stuck. Come higher in every area. More prayer then comes more power. This is my sacred place in you that I shall develop. You shall pray from the depth of your bowels. Pray in all things. Pray that my lightness devours all darkness. Don't ponder, just pray. Don't procrastinate, just pray. Don't remain in a dark place. **Let praying be your guiding light. Pray my daughter.**

August 12

Pray with fervency and compassionately in all things. When the established wouldn't come, the lame, mame, blind and halted came to ME. Prayer will pull the established as well as the frail. Pull consistently in prayer. You can never see what I see but have your eyes open in expectancy. I will grace you with vision as you pray continually. **In your prayers, I want to come in your midst and be released unto you. Pray my daughter.**

August 13

Why not pray? Why not get in my presence to get what you need? Why entertain doubt? Why let uncleanliness bind you? When you pray, the atmosphere is set for my manifestation. When you pray, I visit exactly where you are. As a matter of fact, I emerge forth because I am always present. Pray. Everyone's journey is different. **Pray and expect ME. Pray my daughter.**

August 14

Pray more daily. Don't be stagnated in prayer but put your prayers in motion. You don't want to get stuck pondering. You want to be overtaken in prayer. In praying you're calling on ME and trusting ME. You must pray and believe ME. Pray and let my purging come forth. Prayer produces great changes if you allow it. **Pray my daughter and rest assured that I see you through my eyes of compassion.**

August 15

Pray, pray, pray. Who takes a break from praying? No one should. This should be one of your most aggressive weapons in your midst. Whatever tries to linger or creep in that's not of God, you can attack in prayer. Keep your prayer guard on. Wear it in the good seasons and the bad seasons. Don't be moved out of prayer but be fierce in prayer. Whatever tries to attack your faith, annihilate it with fiery and fervent prayers. Open your mouth wide and let my holy words proceed from you. **Pray my daughter. Pray.**

August 16

My hands are present. As you sup with ME, I'll release you. You are not just praying with mere words but in your prayers you're finding your destination in ME. It's crucial to be seated in ME. Praying reaches continually. Areas you think aren't important, I'm present pushing you in prayer. **Pray my child. Pray.**

August 17

Watch and pray. Pray and watch. This next level is bringing elevation for the entire church. Some will come. Some will resist. Compel all. Pray in intense heat and pray in the coolness of the day. I need for your prayer life to keep launching. When it seems strange, pray. When it's high time, pray. **Pray my daughter, pray and watch the fire grasp all in your midst.**

August 18
PRAYING.

August 19
In your prayers see my word take root and manifesting in your life. Prayer comes in and set the order. Prayer comes in with instructions. Prayer comes in for you to proceed as I speak. In prayer you accept my righteousness and choose nothing less. Prayer destroys every plot and negative force of Satan. Don't pray in fear but pray knowing my peace shall remain. **Pray my daughter. Pray and don't be detoured at all.**

August 20
Praying purges you in all. I'll show you more of yourself in prayer. Some give in to flesh but let my Spirit overtake you. This happens as you have that persistent prayer life. In prayer I am overtaking you with my compassion. Show my love to others. As you pray, something will simmer, and some things regress. Either way in praying, you will know. **Pray my daughter. Pray.**

August 21
Why not pray? It's your life line. It's the umbilical to your nutritional life. It's the place where I make life impartations. It's the place where I speak and your response is, Yes Lord

with no hesitation. You will never forget my manifestation. Pray and you'll see change. Pray and believe and I will call the impossible into your midst. Moses removed himself from the complainers and listened carefully to ME. **Pray my daughter and don't be moved.**

August 22

Pray and watch my release. My word is stronger than your vision. My word goes out and create before you think upon. Whatever it looks like, prayer must supersede your seeing. Elijah was in a famine but he heard the rain. As you pray expect beyond your seeing. Some eyes become diluted and never see again. **I expand your seeing to receive more. Pray my daughter.**

August 23

Pray and expect ME. Afflictions comes but I am forever present. Pray and listen. Pray and receive. Pray and digest. Pray and expect nothing less of my word. Some choose not to pray. That's their choice. I always want to be your first choice. **Pray my daughter and let not Satan enter in. Pray my daughter.**

August 24

Lunge forth strongly in prayer. My time of deliverance rains and always end in the outpouring. Let prayer proceed everything in your midst. Pray and watch my healing power prevail. Whatever healing you need, shall come forth in your preserving prayer. When you open your mouth conquering power comes forth. **Watch, expect, and go back and pray again. Pray my daughter.**

August 25

Anywhere you go, there should be a breakthrough in prayer. Always be my instrument of prayer. Praying clears the way for my complete reign. Pray that prayer warriors will come forth and not settle. You have to be one that will persevere. Others have their assignments you stay on track with yours. Let prayer be your first nature in all things. **Pray my daughter. Compel others to get into their place of miracle-manifestating prayer.**

August 26

Prayer sets you up to walk in greatness. In all things, continue to pray. You should always call on my name. Your victory is in my midst. Praying sets an explosion off where you are. **Pray and watch my supernatural overtake all your situations. Pray my daughter and watch.**

August 27

My power comes forth when you pray my word and stand upon my word. Believe ME with your all when you pray. I want complete assurance in ME as you pray. The enemy wants to stagnate you but I want you to flourish in your confessions. Speak to ME continually for I'm present and reigning and await your call. **Pray my daughter. Pray.**

August 28

Pray and I will give you divine instructions. I'm manifesting through your prayers. Prayer prepares you and then directs you towards the greater. As soon as I awake you, pray and hesitate not. If you pray expecting ME, I'll show up. If you procrastinate then you really have no expectation of ME. Pray and prepare then start over again. **Pray my daughter. Pray. My ears are open to thine cry.**

August 29

Praying will give you conquering strength over every mountain. Praying will lift you from every valley. Praying keeps you moving forward. Be pushed in prayer. When you're praying go harder and use my words aggressively. I expect your prayers to reach ME. **Push hard in your prayers that deliverance will come forth. It may seem like it's your last wind. Keep praying. Pray my daughter. Pray.**

August 30

Your ordained journey is to be my prayer warrior. I expect you to pray. I expect you to call on ME at all times. I shall teach you to be my ferocious prayer warrior. Some pray in the storm and some pray in the sun. I want you to pray regardless. In knowing my word, don't ever let it get away from thine mouth. **Pray my word, sing my word. Let my word be visualized in you. Pray my daughter. Pray.**

August 31

There is a prayer link that I have with my intercessors. Give your all in praying unto ME. What can you change? What can you remove? I am the one you call regardless. Let your breath be consumed in calling on my name. I expect you to trust ME with thine whole heart. **You shouldn't fear what you can't change. Pray my daughter. Pray and give your all as you pray.**

September 1

I hear the cry of my children. It's my commandment for you to pray and trust ME. Pray without doubt always. Have a close encounter in ME. Don't let anything stop your prayers. Pray intensely. Pray in belief. Pray without wavering. Pray and listen for my voice. **Pray my daughter. Pray. Expect ME.**

September 2
PRAYING.

September 3
In all things, in all things, seek ME in prayer. Prayer should never be a second option. Declare my word and never let up from it. If you're delighting in ME, you do have access to the fulfillment of all of your needs. Your prayers should be released with a continual love. Some don't know to pray but you pray and encourage others to pray fervently. **You help mightily as you pray in all things.**
Pray my daughter.

September 4
Prayer pushes. Prayer prevails. Prayer empowers. Prayer pleads your purpose. When you rise, whatever comes, submit it to prayer. The Spirit searches the deep things and I want my prayers from you to go deep. **Don't be stunted in prayer. Pray my daughter and teach others to pray.**

September 5
As you pray you must be assured of my presence. You must pray knowing my word shall manifest. You should take delight in praying and let it be a part of your all. In your prayers keep a thankfulness unto ME. Reverence ME for the release of my answers. Whatever comes, begin and end with prayer. **Pray my daughter for it is a time to pray without ceasing.**

September 6
Pray continually. As you pray, expect. You can be casual in your expectations. Pray and trust ME with your all. Praying keeps

you walking in my obedience. As much as you believe for others, know that I am answering prayers in your midst. Your prayers come to ME. Release them in reverence and not in fear. I have called you to this place of intercession. **Pray, my daughter. Pray and intercede for the greater shall reign.**

September 7

Prayer challenges you to come higher and do more. Prayer guides you and takes you to sealed doors. I expect you to pray and pull the feeble. You live in prayer. Teach others to come forth in this place of habitation. **Prayer should be your residence. Pray my daughter. Pray.**

September 8

Stay in surrendered prayer. In this fast I shall take you to a higher dimension of prayer. Every conversation that comes shall be triggered for you in prayer. I want you to pray and not hold back. I want you to pray with your deepest cry. Pray and watch my power prevail. Pray and let my consuming fire overtake you. **There is another level of prayer. Come ye in. Pray my daughter. Pray.**

September 9

In praying press through for the greater. In praying don't get comfortable. Pray and be moved to my greater. Every time you pray there should be an experience in ME. Praying is that intimate time where your whole heart merges forth. Some things you cannot speak about but you can bring them to the prayer altar. **Pray, my daughter and don't let up. It's a time to intercede greatly.**

September 10

Pray and trust ME. Pray and look upon ME. Pray and expect ME. Pray and acknowledge ME in all things. Praying gives you continual strength. Praying provides for your every need. Prayer leads you, and elevates you on all things. **Praying is for strength and the strong. Pray, my daughter and faint not.**

September 11

As you pray to ME, I'll give you exactly what you need. I shall bring a great release to you. Pray in reverence and great fervency and I'll give you the necessary tools. In all your counsel teach others to fast and pray. If they use those principles, they will be conquerors. Don't use formality in prayer, just pray. **In your prayers I'll show you specifics to target. Pray my daughter. Pray.**

September 12

You must pray and expect. How can you go forth in warfare and not expect ME? You have to be totally dependent upon ME? Your wisdom is to trust ME and not try to analyze ME. That's a waste. Declare ME. Stand on ME. Keep ME in your mouth. You know my capabilities, keep praying. Rejoice in your prayers and never loose heart. **Pray, my daughter for my ears are attentive to your cries.**

September 13

In your prayers, you are compelling the lost. You are sending spiritual directions to their wayward journey. In prayer whether you see the manifestation or not, keep praying. It's crucial to pray before you release. Don't be moved by anyone else, know that I have called you to this place of intercession. Listen my daughter and pray. **I am equipping you to be my warrior in intercession. Pray, my daughter pray.**

September 14

In your prayers you have to believe my word. I know what's on the inside of you and I need my words to manifest through you. Your prayers can be hindered when you don't believe. You pray because you believe ME for change. Encourage others to pray. Direct them to my word. **Pray my daughter and let my rain be continual in your midst. I come for my word.
Pray my daughter.**

September 15

Come and let my word be magnified in you. Praying pulls you and take you to my greater. It's my gift that I released you to pray. Pray and press. Pray and reach. Pray and RECEIVE my continual IMPARTATION. More than anything you must know that I am calling you forth to pray. In ME you will receive the abundance. **Pray, my daughter pray and don't let up.**

September 16

Pray with the deepness of heart. Pray looking for the promised land. Keep praying and never doubt my word of replenishing. Pray and surrender to my every word. My word directs you in the storm and fire. I am erupting, break forth in intense prayer. **You are my intercessor. Be not removed from my feet.
Pray my daughter.**

September 17

In prayer you have to expect ME. Pray and I'll intreat my ear unto you. Every time my Spirit nudges you to pray, pray without hesitation. In one day, I can speak release and it shall manifest before your eyes. Come into my presence for it is your safety. **Be thou cleansed and elevated in ME. Pray my daughter.**

September 18

In each prayer, look into ME. You are calling on my name and should expect my release. I come to my name. Rejoice that my ears are attentive. Rejoice in knowing my prayers are precious to ME. Encourage others to pray and seek ME in all things. Reach greater in prayer. Expect always in prayer. Whatever you see pray and keep praying. **Pray my word and look for it to come off the pages.**

September 19

Speak ME all the days of thine life. Seek and expect knowing I hear the cry of my children. In prayer you're not listening to others but yearning for my response. As soon as I put someone in your spirit, pray. Prayer reaches. When you're in the furnace pray, for I am in control of the temperature. **My word rises you above the heat. Pray my daughter with fervency and sincerity. Pray my daughter.**

September 20

In your prayers release every weight and circumstance. I have no respect of people. The cries come up to ME and I dispatch angels of solutions. Pray beyond your needs and see the great despair of others. Keep the burden upon you to seek ME and call diligently upon ME. Your sincerity comes before ME in all things. My righteousness rains. Hear the rain for its coming in great abundance. **Pray, my daughter. Pray and don't you ever look back. Step into your intercessor's calling.**

September 21

Always enter into prayer with expectation. You take delight in conversing as I communicate to you. Have your ears open and be alert. Watch and pray and then begin again. I challenge you, keep striving for more. **Pray and compel others to come up higher in prayer. Pray, my daughter. Pray.**

 II. SUMMER

*Date:*_____

Prayer Notes: _____
_____
_____
_____
_____
_____
_____

*Date:*_____

Prayer Notes: _____
_____
_____
_____
_____
_____
_____

*Date:*_____

Prayer Notes: _____
_____
_____
_____
_____
_____
_____

Date:_____

Prayer Notes:_____
_____
_____
_____
_____
_____
_____

Date:_____

Prayer Notes:_____
_____
_____
_____
_____
_____
_____

Date:_____

Prayer Notes:_____
_____
_____
_____
_____
_____
_____

*Date:*_____

Prayer Notes: _____
_____
_____
_____
_____
_____
_____

*Date:*_____

Prayer Notes: _____
_____
_____
_____
_____
_____
_____

*Date:*_____

Prayer Notes: _____
_____
_____
_____
_____
_____
_____

*Date:*_____

Prayer Notes: _____
_____
_____
_____
_____
_____
_____

*Date:*_____

Prayer Notes: _____
_____
_____
_____
_____
_____
_____

*Date:*_____

Prayer Notes: _____
_____
_____
_____
_____
_____
_____

FALL

FALL

Yes, I see the Fall! The magnificence of the changing of the leaves and the graceful productive atmosphere. Transition is here.

LET US PRAY

Wonderful and Mighty Savior we adore you. We marvel at the magnificence of the changing leaves and the graceful and productive atmosphere that surrounds us. We recognize that transition is here.

Lord, we adore you for who you are—majestic, righteous, and holy. You are our ALL, and we are grateful for your presence in our lives. Our deepest desire is to represent you and to be actively involved in building your kingdom here on Earth. We stand before you, ready and willing to be molded and transformed into your purged vessels.

We are ready to walk in obedience to your divine guidance. We firmly declare that we will not return to our old ways or to the things that hinder our growth in you. We ask that you empower us to walk according to your will and to carry out your purposes. As we move forward in this season of change, we lovingly say, "Yes, Lord, we hear your call."

May our lives bring glory to your name as we conform to your image. In Jesus' name, we pray.
Amen.

III. FALL

"There was such a glory over everything; the sun came like gold through trees, and over the fields, and I felt like I was in Heaven."
–Harriet Tubman

September 22

When you're in prayer look closely. Hear and not be disturbed in what I reveal. Pray and I'll give you, my directions. Encourage others to pray with there all. Encourage others to call ME diligently. See as much as you pray I'll entrust my gifts unto you. The harvest is coming in, don't stop praying.

Your prayers are watering the seed to come up plentifully. **Pray my daughter. Pray.**

September 23

Pray already seeing the victory. Don't pray trying to come out of defeat but pray knowing you have won in ME. Don't waiver, don't squirm. Stay confident in ME. When you pray with others, you're in total agreement that I'll meet their needs. Be just as confident as you call out to ME for yourself. Encourage the fragile to go forth in steadfast prayer. **Pray my daughter and stand only on what I have said. Pray.**

September 24

Look for ME in your fervent prayer. Why would you pray and not expect? Why would you pray and not believe? I have called you to intercession. I have called you to go forth diligently. As I speak, hold on. See my words walking through your life. Pray, I am delivering. **Pray and never let Satan close your mouth!! Pray, my daughter. Pray.**

September 25

In your prayers listen attentively. I am teaching you, that you may encourage others. Many times, your prayers turn into tears as you ponder on my miracle working power. Always keep thankfulness in your heart. Be encouraged in your light afflictions, knowing that I am God and Savior. Who told you to not trust ME? The one who can never have another opportunity with ME. **Pray, my daughter. Pray.**

September 26

Pray in my power. Don't be weakened in weights but be strengthened in my voice. In my words comes your conquering strength.

It's urgent to pray always. Not just in convenience nor in a preferred season, but to remain in fervent prayer. In all things pray and stand. This is the place where I release the most to you. **Pray and receive my mighty name. My children expect ME. Pray, my daughter. Pray.**

September 27

Pray and doubt not. When you come to ME, be assured that I'm present. You can't come to ME doubting my presence. In your prayers not only am I guiding you spiritually but indeed naturally. Many things shall be released to you because of your location. Divine intervention shall be crucial as you begin to launch in this new direction. **Every time the enemy wants you to stop prayer, go harder and stronger. Pray my daughter.**

September 28

As I reveal, remain in fervent prayer. I have entrusted my seeing unto you. Handle it with care. Walk in love with my revelation. Some will come out through the love and kindness you show. Some will be snatched out. Some will be scared out and some will continue in disobedience. Pray for them all. **As you pray, you must see my word abound in your midst. Pray, my daughter. Pray.**

September 29

Push intensely in prayer. Push with my word. Let it always break forth from your lips. Push in vision. Seeing my word and knowing its manifesting on your behalf. You can't expect for anyone to push on your behalf. I told you to seek ME while I shall be found. Everything about you must be fully engulfed in prayer. **Pray always. Pray in the midst of... just pray.**

September 30

Pray in my power. In the midst of your prayers, you must see my victory. You must see my greatness manifesting in your midst. My word isn't subject to prevail but it always prevails. Always have room for ME and to expand in you. I don't ever want to be limited. Pray with fervency and watch.
Pray, my daughter. Pray.

October 1

Prayer and praise combined yields a powerful force. Pray without hesitation, being assured of my delivering power. Pray immediately that my blessings will fall on my soldiers. Keep prayer in your mouth and the enemy can't enter into your heart. I have called you to intercede. It is where I have called you. Some may forsake the call. Stay surrendered to the task.
Pray my daughter and don't be weakened.
Pray, my daughter. Pray.

October 2

Pray in my power and in my might. You are strengthened in ME. Pray when there are shallow waves and pray when there are raging waters. I need prayer to be an aroma that proceeds out of you. Paul had power for he was always in my presence. My presence is your place of refuge. This place is where you come to be revived in ME. Pray assured that I have given you conquering power. **Pray, my daughter. Pray. For this is the month of many manifestations.**

October 3

Pray unto ME. I hear your outcry to ME. Expect ME. I have called you to this place to have a yearning for souls.

You see beyond the person and see the deliverance for the soul. Pray and speak my oracles. You are my vessel. Pray and watch deliverance come forth and my spirit consume. **Pray my daughter and expect ME in greatness.**

October 4

Elijah prayed for closure and opening. His prayers were earnest toward ME. Never pray out of routine but because I am upon your heart. I hear the cry of my children and purpose shall be fulfilled. Be in that place where you can see ME close and shut. Elijah prayed just like you do. **Pray my daughter and don't be turned around. Pray.**

October 5

You are my intercessor. Open your mouth. Take delight in speaking in speaking my oracles. Many are frail in your midst, pray and speak. Life is being resuscitated back into their bodies as you speak my words. Focus and have compassion on others but most importantly on what I have called you to do. As you pray be intrigued at what I say and take delight in my commandments. **Pray my daughter and compel the lost in prayer. Pray my daughter and hesitate not.**

October 6

Prayer purges and bringeth forth purity. As soon as you pray, I want you to see the turnaround of the answer. As soon as you pray don't give doubt a lingering moment. Be assured of ME. Pray daughter and expect. Pray daughter and release. Pray daughter and never compromise. Pray daughter and declare my word in every breath. **Pray and watch ME prevail in your midst. Praying is not for doubters.**

October 7

Heeding to ME in prayer brings continual victory. I want you to pray fervently and obey always. Some don't pray because of the instructions to follow. Pray and hear ME. Pray and abide in ME. Pray and watch an outpouring of my spirit. Pray and have an experience in ME. Pray and yield. Pray and be surrendered. Don't stop praying. Pray and believe. **Pray my daughter. Pray.**

October 8

Prayer makes you invisible before the enemy. This is a communication like no other. Be excited to receive your IMPARTATION. As you walk in ME, your prayers will abound. Many things you don't have to analyze just pray. As people talk, pray. As people look, pray. Stay in prayer and walk in my Holy Ghost boldness. **Pray my daughter. Pray. Then look for my rain from heaven.**

October 9

See ME as you call upon my name. Pray and listen. Pray and cast your cares upon ME. Pray and allow my righteousness to come forth freely. Some don't see the Need to pray but it's essential for survival. Rejoice, knowing that I am dispatching Angels. Pray, believe and expect. **Pray my daughter. Pray.**

October 10

Pray and be my vessel. You are my unique vessel and operate as I called you. When you don't pray, you find yourself wandering. I have an ordained journey before you. Walk therein going forth in fervent prayer. Some pray in seasons. Pray regardless in extreme delight. I hear my children that seek ME. I am calling you too greater. Seek ME. **Pray my daughter. Pray.**

October 11

Pray and be persistent in your belief. Pray and rejoice for I sitteth in heaven and do whatsoever I please. Pray like you know whom you belong to. Pray and watch my power come forth. Walk in assurance of my Holy Ghost power. I have given you my best. **Pray my daughter. Pray.**

October 12

These are not casual prayers out of routine but prayers that reach my throne room. As your eyes are fixed upon ME, I'm taking care of your concerns. Focus on my word and what it says. The lady pressed to touch ME and that has to be daily in your all. Press and keep pressing. The more you come in my midst, the more I will rain upon you. Never an umbrella is needed. I take delight in you bringing your all to the altar. **Pray my daughter and stay.**

October 13

Let it be ME in you in prayer. Drown everything else out that your focus is on ME. I'll consume you completely. Pray. Believe. See! Don't see the negative. See the impossible. See my delivering. Pray for delivering rain as you call ME. Encourage and release my words of life. As you pray, rejoice. **Pray my daughter. Pray.**

October 14

Stay in steadfast prayer. As you pray declare my word and expect my manifestation. I told you the tenth month was for manifestation. Expect, expect nothing less. Prayer forms the bridge for you to cross over all: raging waters, high tides, venomous beasts. Regardless use the bridge of prayer to cross over. Compel saints to pray and sit in my presence. They build their relationship as they sit in ME. **Pray my daughter. Pray and don't be uprooted.**

October 15

Rise to pray. Men ought to always pray and faint not. Pray without hesitation. It's what I called you to do. You are my intercessor. Proceed with caution declaring my word. Give my words back to ME. My children will not lack but will receive my abundance. Pray in every season. Pray with great delight. **Pray my daughter. Pray.**

October 16

Pray. Prepare. Pray. Prevail. Keep praying and receive of my presence. In seeking ME I'll give you the necessary guide. I'll take you to my destination. Hinder not the journey. Compel the fragile to pray with their whole heart. Prayer allows ME to live in you and my word to purge your all. In all things pray and keep praying. **Pray my daughter. Pray.**

October 17

Pray. Allow my words to come forth from you. And believe ME. As it comes out of your mouth, stand firmly in ME. Encourage people to pray. As you pray, see ME and what I'm raining.

My blood was shed that you may have continual access to ME. All have access but refuse to come to the surrendered place. **Pray my daughter and don't let up. Pray my daughter.**

October 18
In your prayers let ME come forth through you. Pray believing. Pray seeing. Pray intensely. Pray my word. Pray without doubt. Pray declaring. Pray receiving. Your intercession shall go up to greater. I came to Mary because she was available. Always give ME access to your temple. There are places where people want to keep ME out. Give ME full access in all things. **Pray my daughter. Pray.**

October 19
Prayer takes you through every heated situation. It's not always for you to run from the heat but to endure at times, to be elevated. Praying works powerful with your belief. When you call your child, you expect them to come. As you abide in ME, I make visitations. Be disciplined that you may see and receive of ME. **Stay on task and pray my daughter pray.**

October 20
Keep your heart open and bless ME continually. Pray and see ME intensely. Pray and trust ME with your all. Don't stop praying. As I speak heed without hesitation. When people say pray, pray right then and there. You are putting seeds of prayer in the ground and you shall receive lifelong prayers on your behalf. **Pray my daughter. Pray.**

October 21

Can you seek ME, pray and release all? Hold nothing back. I want it all. For in giving ME your all, you will be able to worship ME in spirit and in truth. The disconnections comes when you don't give ME all. Choose my word regardless. Accept ME and expect ME. Satan desires to sift you as wheat but I prayed that your faith will fail you not. Whatever it looks like pray. Whatever try to bind your thoughts, pray. My daughter pray, and stay in your place of surrenderance.

Pray my daughter. Pray.

 III. FALL

*Date:*_____

Prayer Notes: _____
_____
_____
_____
_____
_____
_____

*Date:*_____

Prayer Notes: _____
_____
_____
_____
_____
_____
_____

*Date:*_____

Prayer Notes: _____
_____
_____
_____
_____
_____
_____

*Date:*_____

Prayer Notes: _____
_____
_____
_____
_____
_____
_____

*Date:*_____

Prayer Notes: _____
_____
_____
_____
_____
_____
_____

*Date:*_____

Prayer Notes: _____
_____
_____
_____
_____
_____
_____

 III. FALL

*Date:*_____

Prayer Notes: _____
_____
_____
_____
_____
_____
_____
_____

*Date:*_____

Prayer Notes: _____
_____
_____
_____
_____
_____
_____
_____

*Date:*_____

Prayer Notes: _____
_____
_____
_____
_____
_____
_____
_____

*Date:*_____

Prayer Notes: _____
_____
_____
_____
_____
_____
_____

*Date:*_____

Prayer Notes: _____
_____
_____
_____
_____
_____
_____

*Date:*_____

Prayer Notes: _____
_____
_____
_____
_____
_____
_____

WINTER

WINTER

Winter whips in with a fierce coldness. Spiritually cold seasons in our lives can be represented by loneliness, despair, and even grief. This may be a season that you have to push through with the tender mercies of God. He is always present to warm our heartaches and bring forth a needful deliverance.

LET US PRAY

Lord, our Loving Savior, help us. We need you. We take comfort in knowing that even in these challenging times, your tender mercies are here to sustain us. We recognize that the unexpected circumstances of life can be overwhelming, but we place our trust in you, for you are faithful. You see our tears, fears, and regrets, and we surrender them to you.

Teach us, O Lord, to lean on you in every season of our lives. Guide us, that regardless of what we face, your Word remains powerful and never diminishes. We are grateful for your constant presence, and we rely on your name for strength and comfort. As we bring our petitions before you, we repeat with persistence, "Yes, Lord, I hear your call," and we eagerly wait for your manifestation in our lives.

We thank you, Lord, for your unfailing love and the assurance that you are with us in the midst of our Winter season. Renew our spirits and grant us the perseverance to push through until the dawn of a new season. In Jesus' name, we pray.
Amen.

IV. WINTER

"YOUR SUCCESS IS IN YOUR ROUTINE."
-Apostle Dr. Oliver Leaks

October 22

Pray and release. In your prayers allow ME to free you. You will be limited in your prayers when you are bound. In your freedom you can pray without limitations. Offer prayer in all things. Prayer is some last resort, but I always want it to be your first. When I was in the garden of Gethsemane I prayed heavily. I prayed and I was able to complete my task.
Be free in ME my daughter and pray.

October 23

Prayer and praise are a combination that steals the enemy. Combine these two in your all. Be raised in prayer. Push to the greater. As you pray say the word, see the word and receive of my word. My word is for you. Keep praying and keep watching. The flesh is weak but the spirit is willing. **Keep praying that all flesh will be subjected to my will. Pray my daughter.**

October 24

Dismantle doubt and everything else that tries to stagger your prayer. As I elevate you in prayer you must walk with ME in every season. Pray in the authority of my word. Your job is to confess it and believe it. I shall manifest it for it belongs to ME. Why pray and not believe? Believe and declare. Believe and hear. Pray my daughter. **Pray in ME and not in doubt.**

October 25

Pray and receive. Pray and expect. Pray without hesitation. When you pray to ME with your whole heart I hear and respond. As you pray, lay before ME and let ME impart unto you. Prayer leads you into the greater. When people ask you to pray; do it on the spot. **Prayer thrusts you forth and keeps you from being overtaken. Pray my daughter. Pray.**

October 26

Pray, pray, pray. Then keep coming back to pray. See my word taking hold entirely as you pray. Praying is always your place of safety and assurance. Pray through every fiery dart and be strengthened in my word. Your power comes from ME as you go forth in prayer. Pray and doubt not for I AM able. **Pray my daughter. Pray.**

October 27

Your prayers are first, your prayers are throughout the day. Your prayers are continual. Keep praying and stay surrounded at the altar. Greatness is here and it is preceded from my altar. **Open your eyes in full capacity and see my glory revealed. Pray my daughter, pray and then go back and pray. I love you my child.**

October 28

Prayer is what you have heard. Prayer is what you have learned. Prayer comes from the deepness of your soul. Prayer is what's manifested before your eyes. Whatever it looks like, keep praying. Let it overflow from you. See the need and go forth in intercession regardless. I have entrusted you to pray. **Pray my daughter.**

October 29

Pray and rejoice in my Holy Ghost. I am presently outpouring in to your mind, body and soul. As you pray believe and defeat doubt. Doubt destroys the harvest of seeds designated for your abundance. The storms may be raging and your pain may seem unbearable but as you pray, I will make a way of destiny. Pray with your earnest heart in full expectations. Teach others to pray and be assured in my word. **Pray my daughter. Pray. I love you.**

October 30

In your prayers look wholly upon ME. Your answers are always in my word. Praying gives you the power and persistence to keep moving. Truly believe in my power and nothing less. Pray, believe, and then receive of my instructions. Some come in prayer, hopeless. But if you enter in and have an encounter with ME, life changes shall come forth. **Pray, my child, and stand strong and let my word be activated in you. Pray my daughter.**

October 31

Prayer in this month has brought forth manifestation. You have to pray and look. You have to pray and believe. Prayer has gaining power. Be not judgmental but stay in continual prayer. Let your opinion be factual according to my words. Encourage others to pray. As you pray, you're experiencing ME in your body. **Pray my daughter and keep praying.**

November 1

So many things are attached to your prayer life. It's an urgency for continual prayer. Some flames barely flicker because they don't give ME access in prayer. I walk in you when you're surrendered in prayer. I hear your cries and yearnings. Hear my instructions and obey. **Trust and follow with the joy of the Lord. Pray my daughter. Pray.**

November 2

Quench not my Spirit and be surrendered. I am calling forth a cry from your yearnings. As you see, stay on your knees. As change manifests, stay on your knees. Stay in continual prayer for countless victories. Prayer should be priority but some don't chose it first. Be strengthened as you lay out in prayer. Prayer elevates and strengthens you at the same time. **Pray my daughter pray and expect!**

November 3

This has been the assignment; 6 months of prayer journaling. Continue to go forth in ME in mighty prayer. I will give you my divine order in releasing this knowledge. Never lose your reverence in prayer. Pray in every season. Pray down to your last breath. Pray with your whole heart. Keep praise and prayer attached securely. Instruct others to pray. Listen and heed.
Pray my daughter. Pray.

*Date:*_____

Prayer Notes: _____
_____
_____
_____
_____
_____
_____

*Date:*_____

Prayer Notes: _____
_____
_____
_____
_____
_____
_____

*Date:*_____

Prayer Notes: _____
_____
_____
_____
_____
_____
_____

*Date:*_____

Prayer Notes: _____
_____
_____
_____
_____
_____
_____
_____

*Date:*_____

Prayer Notes: _____
_____
_____
_____
_____
_____
_____
_____

*Date:*_____

Prayer Notes: _____
_____
_____
_____
_____
_____
_____
_____

Date:_____

Prayer Notes: _____
_____
_____
_____
_____
_____

Date:_____

Prayer Notes: _____
_____
_____
_____
_____
_____

Date:_____

Prayer Notes: _____
_____
_____
_____
_____
_____

In Closing, my heart-felt desires that as you've embellished upon this prayer journey that you have learned the critical significance of laying before the Lord. Being in His presence is costly; it costs your time yet raises you to greater elevations, ultimately preparing you for your final destination in glory. As we enter into His presence, let us stay in unison that our response to his will shall be, YES LORD, I HEAR YOUR CALL.

LET US PRAY….

Father, in the mighty name of Jesus, we come repenting of our sins. Lord we ask in the mighty name of Jesus that you would cleanse us and teach us your will.
Our yearnings are to know more about you and the importance of spending time with you.
We honor you and bless your name for being our Creator, our Healer, our Deliverer, OUR EVERYTHING.
Lord, everyday as we pursue our daily tasks let us place nothing before you. You are Mighty and our Magnificent Savior.
We are here daily to exalt your Holy and Righteous name.
Help us Lord, that we are never too busy to sit at your feet and always take lovingly hold of your glorious word. Your purity and your goodness engulfs us daily and we are grateful to be your children. Life can be amazing yet have challenges but our yearnings is to know about you.
Help us Lord to sit in your presence and release our all.
As we pray and look unto you, our promises back unto you will be YES LORD, I HEAR YOUR CALL!
Thank you Lord, in the mighty name of Jesus we pray.
AMEN

A Note from the Author
Dr. Deirdre Leaks

We are all of God's creation. He created mankind to worship and praise him. Amidst rendering our all to him, he speaks. Whether it's to our heart, through his words or through his chosen vessels, He speaks. It's vital that we receive His divine oracles. His impartations are necessary in fulfilling the ordained call upon our individual lives.

Daily I arise between 2:30 am - 3:00 am to bask in the presence of the Lord. It's a beautiful time where I lay prostrate before him for a couple of hours and pour out my heart to him. It is so personal and I experience Him mightily. If your daily time is in the morning, noon or evening, GIVE HIM TIME! CALL UPON HIS NAME, for his ears are open.

"Evening, and morning, and at noon, will I pray, and cry aloud: and he shall hear my voice."
-Psalm 55:17

Yes Lord, I Hear Your Call; came to me as I laid in his presence. Many things are birthed as we sit in him. He spoke and I responded, YES LORD! Prayerfully this will encourage you to realize the importance of honoring our mighty Savior by sitting in him. You may begin with five minutes then progress to longer times. Whatever the case may be, just willing to answer,

YES LORD, I HEAR YOUR CALL!

About the Author

Deirdre Michelle Dukes-Leaks accepted the Lord Jesus Christ as her Savior as a teenager in May 1988. Almost after 35 years later, she lovingly proclaims JESUS as her King of King and Lord of Lords. Throughout her glorious life changing journey, she stands dependently upon the word of God. She is steadfast in prayer and assured that God's best is for His children. In 2017 after going to the E.R. for stomach cramps, she had a miraculous encounter from the Lord. After six days in the hospital and two major surgeries, she experienced JEHOVAH ROPHA, in magnificence. She declares, continually, trust God, He will take care of you.

As a youth, Deirdre was heavily involved in church. Her participation ranged from youth choir, praise team, Sunday school and church delegate. Deirdre is tremendously grateful to be the wife, of the Anointed and awesome vessel of God, Apostle Dr. Oliver Leaks, Jr. He is the Outstanding Senior Pastor of Fresh Manna Ministries, Barnesville, Ga. Deirdre assists her husband continuously and serves as the church administrator. She is an ordained minister and recently received her Doctorate Degree in Biblical Studies. She also serves on the Intercession team, women's ministry and community outreach. Her desire is to to be a gap-filler and work anywhere there's a need. She gives her all in every capacity. They have been beautifully married for over 35 years and give God all the praise for His hands upon their marriage. God has truly blessed their union and it has been a testimony to countless couples that they encounter. They have three wonderful children and spouses.

The handsome Joshua Leaks; adoring Kiyuna and Charles Williams and Amazing Jakila and Joshua Ransom. Their children diligently serve in diverse aspects of the ministry.

Deirdre has two amazing grandchildren Olivia Grace and Elijah Wesley Williams and anticipate at least 8 more grandchildren. Deirdre tells everyone about the goodness of God. She is known not just to pray for you but will pray with you anywhere. She proclaims everywhere Psalms 8:1 *"O Lord, our Lord, How excellent is Thy name in all the earth! Who has set Thy glory above the heavens."*

I welcome all readers of this book to connect with me on Social Media

FACEBOOK: Deirdre Leaks

INSTAGRAM: @DeirdreLeaks

Additional Copies of this book may be purchased at all major retailers including:

Acknowledgements:

First of all, I give glory to My Lord and Savior Jesus Christ. Thank you for being my everything and allowing me to be a part of your kingdom. I am forever grateful that you are ABBA FATHER! You are my King and I'm honored to be your servant. I'm sincerely humbled that you've entrusted me with such a great task. *All the glory belongs to you, O' Lord!*

Wonderful thanks and reverence to my anointed Apostle and life time encourager, my distinguished handsome husband, Apostle Dr. Oliver Leaks, Jr. Thank you for being an awesome leader and supporting me in everything. Your series of teachings on, *Next Level Living*, has thrust me into this new dimension of faith. Thank you for always challenging me outside of my comfort zone and pushing me into excellence. I AM extremely blessed to have you as my leader and thankful that as God imparts into you, that you will continue to disperse unto us. You are the word in action and a great Man of Valor. *I love you for life.*

To our children: Joshua Don Leaks, Kiyuna (Charles) Williams and Jakila (Joshua) Ransom, THANK YOU. Your continued support is amazing! To see you all serve God is extremely uplifting. Each one of you are great and I take delight in seeing the call of God manifest in your lives. Because of your lives, my intercession was maximized and I am blessed for the journey. Thank you for encouraging ME and allowing ME to be your parent. You are my precious jewels. Additional shout out to my personal Marketing Director on this here her first project, Mrs. Jakila Ransom and assistant, Jamori Murphy. *Awesome job!*

Blessings to our beautiful intelligent grandchildren, Olivia Grace and Elijah Wesley Williams; and the many grandchildren to come.

Thank you to those that birthed me into the world, my parents. My magnificent mother, Annette W. Dukes, and my father, William Dukes, Sr. Mom, your resilience and perseverance have been amazing to watch and continues to encourage ME. *Thank you both for your support.*

Blessings to my great siblings: William (Marcee) Dukes Jr. and Selina (John) Walton. *I appreciate your love and support.*

Fresh Manna Ministries, you MIGHTY WARRIORS! Thank you for allowing us to serve you and entrusting your families in our midst. We treasure your love and your continual support. Our lives are better because you all have made a life long impact. Keep trusting the word of God and thriving in His holiness. *His greatness is for you.*

To the greatest mother of the church, Mother Clara Barlow, a blessed and beautiful 84 years old. You are always there with great encouragement. *We love the church and you eternally.*

Bishop Kenneth and the late 1st Lady Gloria Jean Fuller, THANK YOU. You both took me in and ministered to my soul. You opened your homes and shared your lives. You taught me throughly in the scriptures and even allowed me to work in the ministry. God knew what I needed and blessed me with phenomenal leaders. *First Lady is in glory, but my remarkable memories of her remain with ME always.*

In Memory of Apostle Evelyn Ponder, you were a unique vessel of God. Thank you for pushing me into Ministry. You declared it many years ago. Your dedication to fasting and prayer sparked life changes in me. You were also an endearing and encouraging mother-in-law. *Although your'e in glory, you will forever be loved and missed.*

In Memory of Dr. H.L. Morgan, THANK YOU! Dr. Verlene Morgan, you all are amazing, wonderful, and are the Best Overseers. You were always there and I am blessed to have you in my life. Thanks for teaching with your lives and the scriptures. Your guidance and Godly advice has steered me to be more than a conqueror. *We appreciate you both and know, Dr. H.L. Morgan, that you're in glory and loving every moment.*

Chief Apostle Tilden Colton and Pastor Sharnette Colton, you are both great leaders, powerful teachers and loving valuable friends. It has been a superb journey and I always look forward to the fellowship. Thanks for your listening ears, continual Godly impartations, and countless laughs. *You are jewels in my midst.*

Bishop Michael (Iris) Lawrence, thank you both for your lives. Bishop Lawrence, thank you for obeying God and speaking this book into existence. The prophecy you gave in May 2018 ignited the flame in me to proceed with what God had ministered to my heart. *I love you both and am thankful that you are vessels to the Body of Christ.*

Apostle Deborah and Wayne Sheppard, thank you both for being gifts to the kingdom of God. Apostle Deborah, thank you for yielding to the voice of God and confirming the direction of this book through prophecy in March 2020. I was at a standstill but as you spoke, divine direction manifested. *I love you and appreciate your continual encouragement.*

Pastor Stephen and Lady Fernanda Whitaker, THANK YOU! As a teenager you allowed me to see discipleship in action. You both prayed with our family, had bible study with our family, prayed with our family, nurtured our family, lived holiness before our family and then PRAYED, PRAYED AND PRAYED! *You both are PRAYER WARRIOR GENERALS!*

Auntie Pastor Betty Martin and The late Pastor Frank Martin, Sr. *Thank you for your continual love and encouragement.*

A special thanks to my beautiful makeup artist, Pastor Richetta Ponder and the up and rising fantastic photographer, Tobias Terrell.

A co-publishing service for indie authors seeking a strategic bigger partner alliance for greater visibility and success in today's marketplace.

561-990-BOOK (2665)
info@ DivineWorksPublishing.com
www.DivineWorksPublishing.com

YOU WRITE,
WE PUBLISH,
TOGETHER WE CREATE...

www.ingramcontent.com/pod-product-compliance
Lightning Source LLC
Chambersburg PA
CBHW070241090526
44586CB00035B/1373